CREATE!
Idea-rich strategies for enhanced innovation

Bob 'Idea Man' Hooey
Author of, Why Didn't I Think of That?

Create your long-term business success! 2024

Preface

A wise man once told me, **"My ability to earn would be directly dependent on my ability to 'creatively' solve client problems and to help people make better decisions."** I've taken his words to heart and worked diligently to make in my writing and client engagements!

As committed business owners and professionals, we are paid for our ability to **creatively solve our client's problems** by providing services or products. As innovative leaders, managers, owners, sales professionals, or even association executives, 'creativity' and/or innovation is our stock-in-trade as we serve and solve our numerous client and membership needs. The tools, tips, and techniques shared *in* **'CREATE!'** and my **'Why Didn't I THINK of That?'** can be **applied** in at least **three directions:**

- Problem-solving and decision making
- Strategic planning for business and career enhancement
- Tapping your inner genius or Creative S.O.U.L.

It has been my experience that the 'tools', tips, tid-bits, and techniques in this little guidebook will help you in the process of defining the direction and outlining the creative process you need to 'successfully' reach the goals you set for yourself and your respective teams.

These creativity tools are 'essential' in helping you birth your dreams or in solving perplexing problems for your clients/customers and/or members you encounter. They can better help you form, train, and lead your teams.

We created this min-edition with a focus to help fellow leaders blend creativity into their leadership styles; and to assist business owners and managers blend creativity into better attracting and serving their prospective clients and leading their teams. Enjoy!

Table of Contents

Why Didn't I THINK of That?
The creative power of Ideas at Work!

"Leadership," says Peter Drucker **"is lifting a person's vision to higher sights, raising a person's performance to a higher standard, and building a personality beyond its normal limitations."** Now that is <u>creative</u> vision!

The foundations of effective, personal leadership whether in a business, a career, or leading a volunteer group, start with 'each' person actively taking responsibility for their own actions as part of a group. Personal leadership precedes powerful, effective leadership in any role. Those foundations are enhanced in feeling confident enough to suggest, create ideas, and accept revisions in team goals and performance.

You might be asking, *"What does leadership have to do with* **creativity and innovation?"** Quite frankly, everything! If we are to successfully learn new styles of applied problem-solving, unlock our creativity, and increase our ability to make better decisions, more creative decisions; we must be willing to take personal leadership in using them in our own activities and in the interaction with fellow workers, team members, and clients.

"Our productivity – often survival – does not depend solely on how much effort we expend, but on whether or not the effort we invest is in the right direction." We must create visionary, innovative road maps that will guide us and our colleagues to greater success.

Peter Drucker also said, *"Management is doing things right; Leadership is doing the right things."* That means **creating better options to precede our decisions and their implementation**.

Our goal in effectively handling major problems, challenges, and mistakes is being able to cut through to the root causes and then creatively develop real innovative solutions to put into action.

My objective is to assist you in acquiring some new problem-solving models and introducing a few creative nudges and tools that will help you in your personal life, career, and interaction with your clients and co-workers. We will touch on the problem-solving process to creatively outline creative solutions – workable solutions that can be implemented today!

I hope to help you discover a new creative approach and mindset to the problems you may encounter. I challenge you to see them as creative opportunities to grow and change the way you live and/or do business.

Some benefits for enhancing our creativity might be:

- More accurate information – increased productivity through better communication and application of creativity in the workplace.
- Effective coordination of activities – how do I fit in the big picture? Improving the flow of ideas – both internally (up and down) and externally.
- Facilitating the decision-making process – being a creative agent of change.
- Training – cross-training, uniform training, and to provide an interactive forum (time permitting).
- Building morale – encouraging teamwork and mutual support.

Occasionally, we need to 'pause' to gain a higher perspective to make sure we are still heading in the right direction. Our efficiency can be misdirected if we are not going where we want in pursuit of our goals.

In my previous life, I worked as a kitchen designer solving challenges and creating amazing home improvement projects for my clients. I remember driving home to Calgary from Lethbridge, AB early one winter morning. I had been working with Southern Alberta clients all week and wanted to get back into the office early so I could drop off my paperwork, get a bit of catch up done, and start my weekend. I was making good time cruising down the highway with the radio playing some great tunes. Then, I noticed a sign saying Castelgar, BC only 65 miles. Whoa! I pulled over and collected my thoughts. How could that be? I was heading home to Calgary, Alberta! Somehow in my overworked, tired brain I had driven right through Fort Macleod and missed at least two BIG highway signs reminding me to turn 'right' to head 'north' to Calgary. Sure, I was making great time, but I was going in the 'wrong' direction.

One of the biggest lessons I've learned about creative problem solving is: **There is always a solution.** Often, there are **a multitude of solutions.** If your problem is industry specific, you might want to talk to others in your industry and **'Thunder-think'** or brainstorm some answers. Or you might want to bring it to your next Chamber of Commerce, networking, mastermind, or association meeting.

The other lesson learned: **I'm not the 'only' one with a problem. Sharing a problem can lead to solving it.** Someone not directly involved in your problem may see a solution or thread that unravels it, because of the difference in his or her perspective or experience or because they are not emotionally involved!

I remember a story of an elevator being built at the El Cortez hotel in San Diego, CA. The owner and architect were discussing the timing needed to remodel and add another internal one and how long the hotel would be shut down. A janitor overheard and, worried about his job, asked what was happening and why. The architect dismissively asked if he had a better idea. He suggested building it on the outside – the first of its kind in the world. Hmm!

We've written this 'work-in-progress' (*a form of innovation*) specifically to guide you and provide tips, techniques, and creative problem-solving models that work in the real world.

I believe passionately in the information presented and enjoy the opportunity to pass it on to you.

The Six Creative Indicators

Can you tell who is more likely to be a creative addition to your team? Can you separate the 'really' creative from the herd? Well according to research there are six basic indicators that might help in your quest to attract creative people for your team. People who rank high or exhibit more of these characteristics tend to be more creative.

Idea volume and fluency

This is an area where volume 'actually' counts. It may take 30 average ideas to yield one great one. Creative people tend to be better at generating ideas, even if most of them have little long term or applicable commercial value. Our minds are very much like a 'muscle' in that we tend to work better when we warm them up. They work better when they are exercised on a regular basis, too. Our best ideas often come after we have worked through the more basic ones.

Slow to jump to conclusions or judge

You tend to get more high-quality ideas when judgment is withheld. This is the secret to effective brainstorming or **'Thunder-thinking'**. Judging cuts off the creative flow of ideas. Judging tends to look for what doesn't fit or won't work verses exploring possibilities and potential. Creativity is willing to explore the options and potentials.

Imagination and flexibility

Creativity in its essence is based on flexible thinking. Creative people tend to exhibit almost a kid-like curiosity about life. Acting as if the world can be as you imagine enhances your creativity.

"The best way to predict the future is to create or invent it."

Concentration and focus

Both traits are 'critical aspects' of creativity. Concentration is staying focused on a specific subject, even when you are tired, bored or frustrated. Creative behaviors can ignore or tune out distractions and outside stimuli while working to solve a problem or reach a goal. Focus on where you want to go.

Able to deal with ambiguity

Creativity is dealing with the vague and unformed to create the clear and concise. Creative people tend to be able to handle ambiguity where there is no clearly defined right or wrong. Creative people have a willingness to see all sides of a situation and to remain in questioning mode rather than rushing to find the answer. They keep going past the 'first' right answer to explore for the 'best' answer or innovative solution.

Able to handle disorder

Creative people tend to handle or even prefer disorder. Forget the stereotype of the absent-minded professor with stacks all around the office. This may be valid, but **disorder is not necessarily 'mess'**. Disorder refers to non-linear thinking, shaking up the normal order, status quo, or non-symmetrical design.

Keep these six indicators in mind when you are looking to recruit a member of your Mastermind Alliance, sales and marketing team, or support team. People do exhibit their creative traits if you are willing to look at and analyze their behaviour. Remember we can unleash our creativity, too.

"There is no doubt that creativity is the most important human resource of all. Without creativity, there would be no progress, and we would be forever repeating the same patterns." **Edward de Bono**

Change is a creative choice

In life, we often have the 'opportunity' thrust upon us to make changes. A death, a major illness, **or a major economic upheaval** can force us to take stock of our lives at that point and sometimes make radical changes. For example, 9-11 and the 2007-2008 economic melt-down did that for many of us.

In our rapidly changing economy, we find businesses and professional associations being stretched and tested as competition becomes increasingly global. Staffing has become more challenging and so has training and marketing. Clients are becoming more demanding and specific in what they want. Time and resources are constantly being stretched.

Change is pushed on us everywhere we turn. We can't avoid change, can we? That's what too many business owners think and miss their full potential. Even some of the most creative companies can fall behind if they don't continue their path of ongoing innovation and product or service creation.

But isn't it better to seize the opportunities to change and grow? Isn't it better to be open to learn, stretch, and push yourself past your comfort zone? Move into your winner's zone!

This change is a creative choice! Life is a series of changes and choices. Why not control their direction and pace!

"Searching for the peak performer within yourself has one basic meaning – You recognize yourself as a person who was born, not as a peak performer but as a learner. With the capacity to grow, change, and reach for the highest possibilities of human nature, you regard yourself as a person in process. Not perfect, but a person who keeps asking: What more can I be? What else can I achieve that will benefit me and my company? What will contribute to my family and my community?" **Charles Garfield**

Ask yourself these questions. Allow your honest reactions to reflect the changes in your attitudes and actions that may need to be addressed to maximize your life and dealings.

- What do I really want to accomplish in my life? What is my biggest dream or goal?
- What would I like my company to accomplish? Where do I want my career to go?
- What am I afraid of? What is stopping me? What keeps me up at night?
- What do I need to change to make it work? When do I need to change it?
- When will I commit to start making these changes?

Will you have the courage to change? Will you commit to be your best and to creatively build your business or association to maximize its potential?

Remember the words of wisdom from retailer J.C. Penny: *"No one need live a minute longer as he/she is, because the creator endowed us with the ability to change ourselves."*

Answering these questions will have given you a 'glimpse' of what needs to be changed to make your dreams and goals a reality. The secret is in putting foundations under your dreams and actions to your goals.

The secret to **unlocking your 'creativity' potential** is accessing your ability to embrace and use change for mutual benefit. **The choice is yours!**

"Change comes with such rapidity that businesses must anticipate tomorrow's needs today, because the distinction between today and tomorrow is increasingly blurred. Innovation is the way of life, central to how an organization conducts itself, becomes fundamental to corporate survival."
Nicholas Imparato *and* **Oren Harrari**, *from 'Jumping the Curve'*

Business observations on applied creativity

When teaching this program in person I often pull examples from business to illustrate creative techniques. Many of these you know, but they still ring true.

For example, **Barbie** is a creative example of a product with a built-in add-on or up-sell capacity. She comes with one outfit, and you are encouraged to buy more and to accessorize her life. You can even buy her friends too. Interesting!

Dominos built a profitable slice of the pizza business by simply promising to get it there hot and ready to eat. This differentiated them from those cold and greasy competitors. What can you do to differentiate yourself from your competition? What can you create as your unique selling proposition?

Telus, AT&T, and the satellite or cable outlets taught how to take a basic service and bundle items clients want for a higher rate. What can you bundle?

Starbucks took an espresso machine previously seen in Italian and European coffee shops and built and empire around the world selling their 'experience'.

Canadian trapper, **Charles Birdseye** observed that the fish he caught during the winter froze quickly. When he cooked them, they still tasted fresh. This observant concept was the start of the frozen food industry.

Federal Express applied an idea (central hub) used by banks in clearing checks and documents as the basis for an effective and efficient delivery system.

We have many more from recent history that teach us that applied creativity can be very profitable. Uber, Airbnb, etc.

One percent better!

"Excellence results from doing 100 things 1 percent better, rather than one thing 100 percent better."
Author Unknown

One of the biggest obstacles to growth is the 'misguided' quest for the big idea, the big break, the big sale, or the big change. Success, sales, and growth happen one step at a time, one improvement at a time, and often a simple, one percent-at-a-time.

Sure, there are many stories of major breakthroughs and advances; perhaps you've even experienced one or more yourself. However, when you look at what led up to them, you'll often see multiple efforts to improve, research, prepare, and experiment. This is often the case in my life and business as I work and prepare in advance of the successful completion or creative breakthrough.

It would be so easy if we could simply wait until the big million-dollar idea drops into our brains or laps and then reap the benefits. It would also be unrealistic to live that way. It would be like buying a lotto ticket as a means of paying your monthly bills. Top performers and leaders are never fully satisfied with where they or their teams are. They have what many would call *'creative discontent'* in that they can always see ways of tweaking or making it better. Many of the ones I meet or work with live this way.

Peters and Waterman *(In Search of Excellence)* wrote, *"The* essence of excellence is the thousand concrete, minute-to-minute actions performed by everyone in an organization to keep a company on its course."

Sam Walton of Wal-Mart was *famous* for looking at his competition with the eye of learning *'one thing'* he could use to make what he and his team did a bit better. He built a large, successful, multi-national company from a very little one by applying this concept of continuous improvement.

Jack Welsh made some amazing and profitable changes in GE by doing the same thing.

What are your competitors doing better so that you can apply?

Are there 10 to 15 areas where you can make changes that will give you a 1% improvement?

Write the ideas for improvement down and schedule specific time to make them happen.

One percent better can be your rallying call in the pursuit of excellence and success in your leadership, career, or company. Create and then change!

Brain boosters: (take a minute and play with one or two)

Write your name upside down – and backwards! This means you start from the last letter in your name. Notice how this feels.

Make up a list of 'socially acceptable' activities people could do while standing in line.

Draw a picture of a nature scene only using triangles.

A new business magazine has just been created, unlike any others on the market thus far. What is the name of this magazine and what is its focus?

Note: I love these ideas to challenge your brain someone sent to me more than a dozen years ago. Wish I could remember who sent them, so I could give them credit. They are amazing tools to train your brain.

What if?

A few questions to ponder…

What if you could have anything you wanted in life? **What if** you had all the talent, skills, money, and help you needed to accomplish your wildest dreams? **What if** you could find the solution to the challenge you face? **What if** you were really in charge of your life? What would you do? Where would you go? Who would you become? Hmm!

Often, we encounter people mired in the day-to-day reality who have *forgotten how to dream*. People who have had their dreams 'down-sized' by the dream killers among us; or have dreams eroded by the harsh demands of their environment, situation, and their ongoing involvements.

Surprisingly, the **answers we get in life are directly linked to the questions we ask!** Ask the right questions and get different, more creative, more fulfilling answers. Often, we accept the 'obvious answers' and settle for 'seconds' when we could continue to ask for more and in turn receive even more than we'd ever dreamed possible.

This chapter leads you through a few personal questions in a search to see your dreams expanded and grounded. This is the place to let your creative visualization skills run amok. Use soft background music to set the atmosphere for your mind to soar, to explore the possibilities these questions may spark. Keep a piece of paper close at hand to capture 'your' insights.

This is a place where you need to be honest, without judgment; a place to let your imagination loose and explore the possibilities. Later we will cover how to integrate this area into your present-day reality; to begin seeing your dreams take form as you build solid **Foundations for Success** under them.

Relax! Let your mind flow and wrap your imagination around your 'future'!

What if:

1. I was really in charge of my life, I'd: _____
2. I could do anything, without fear of failure, I'd: _____
3. I had enough money to ensure my basic living needs for a year, I'd: _____
4. I discovered I had the talent or could learn the skills I need to: _____, I'd: _____
5. Something I've always wanted to do is: _____
6. IF I could do anything, without limitations, I'd: _____
7. IF spoke as if (I thought) what was saying was important, I'd say: _____
8. I've always wanted to visit: _____
9. I've always wanted to learn to: _____
10. I would like to leave a legacy of: _____
11. IF I could give my family anything, it would be: _____
12. IF I took full responsibilities for my choices, I'd: _____
13. IF I took full responsibility for my actions, I'd: _____
14. IF I were more accepting of: _____, I'd: _____
15. IF I took full responsibilities for my choice of companions, I'd: _____
16. IF I could have any career, without limitations: _____
17. IF I had a dedicated support team to assist me, I'd: _____
18. IF God cared and was willing to help me, I'd: _____
19. My greatest life goal is: _____
20. IF I could accomplish JUST ONE thing before I die, I'd:

_____

By now your mind should be *whirling with endless possibilities*. To explore those possibilities will require a choice of investing time and effort into 'doing your homework'. To research and refine your dreams using these questions to unlock your creative power; begin to dream again and to act on those dreams will take courage and commitment. **It is so worth it!**

Unlock Your Creative Potential

"Ideas are the beginning point of all fortunes."
Napoleon Hill

Unlocking your 'Creative' potential challenges you to draw from the same 'untapped' creative well that allows you to dream, dare, and declare to the world, *"I DO and will make a difference!"*

We will attempt to 'kick-start' your creativity and challenge your mindsets; to look at what you do, who you are, from a fresh perspective. This small 'learning guide' was created to give you some solid ideas to build on in pursuit of that creative and innovative quest.

To truly expand and **Unlock Your 'Creativity' Potential,** explore these ideas:

Learn to tap into your **Creative S.O.U.L.: S**eeker of wisdom; **O**penness to people and ideas; **U**nlimited energy; and a high **L**evel of risk and adventure.

Learn and apply the *creative process* to your situation:
- Preparation
- Incubation
- Illumination
- Implementation or action on your creative thoughts.

Believe in your creative abilities. *Belief precedes creation!*

Don't be afraid to ask 'stupid' questions. There aren't any!

Challenge your assumptions and existing mindsets.

Give your ideas breathing space to germinate and grow.

Read outside your normal zone to expand your mind. *(Try some of my books)*

Mastermind: with a creative, collaborative circle of friends and fellow creative idea seekers.

Travel and be open to explore and expand by truly seeing new ideas.

Learn to explore the World Wide Web. Visit us at: **www.ideaman.net.**

Make a conscientious effort to capture, record, and save your ideas. Then Act!

See your **Ideas At Work!** by using the four critical building blocks: Planning, Passion, Persistence, and of course, Patience to see it through!

Remember to have fun! We learn best in times of enjoyment.

Use 'Thunder-thinking' (brainstorming) to get outside your box.

Create a special place or environment that sparks your creativity.

Share and expect synchronicity with the world.

Encourage idea volume generation with all your connections.

Some quick thoughts that might help you crank up the volume and burst your locked in *'I'm not creative'* bubble.

As Jacob Bronowski wrote, **"The world can only be grasped by action, not by contemplation...The hand is the cutting edge of the mind."**

Creative Freedom

Question everything? Does what you're doing...

+ Provide enhanced 'value' to the product or customer?
+ Improve 'quality'?
+ Improve 'productivity' or directly reduce costs?
+ Improve 'two-way communication'?
+ Improve 'service'
+ Add to employee satisfaction, 'motivation' or morale?
+ 'Empower' your employees to act?
+ Encourage 'innovation'?
+ Speed up the 'decision-making' process?
+ Give customers more 'reasons' to deal with you?
+ 'Free up time' to more productively sell or service?

What if it didn't exist?

Is it already being done by someone else?

Is it a 'valid' tradition? Why?

Can another person, department, or company do it better, faster, less expensively, or more easily?

Principles made personal yield powerful results - Ideas At Work!

Creativity is a survival tool instilled at birth. However, it is a tool that needs to be 'enhanced,' 'honed,' and 'sharpened' as we move forward into life; more so as we enhance our career skills and roles as creative leaders, business owners, and top-level professionals.

Creativity is 99% perspiration and 1% inspiration
"Whoever said it was going to be easy?"

Bryan Mattimore's excellent creativity book, **'99% Perspiration'** should be in your organization's library. Actually, it should be signed out and 'worn out' by both you and your team. This kind of instructive reading would be time well spent preparing and priming your creativity pump. This is where the 'creative' and 'profitable' ideas come from in better serving your clients and expanding your career or business. This is where you create ideas to profitably enhance your productivity.

I've adapted this chapter from our *'Create the Future!* as a sampler and perhaps a 'seed' for your success in finding time to grow your own leadership, team, and organization more productively.

Our ongoing success and survival in business is directly dependent on our 'creative ability' to profitably solve the problems in our client's lives and operations. We use our innovative solutions to help make their lives and businesses better. Accessing or tapping into your creativity will be hard work unless you systemize your approach.

We hear stories of the 'ah-ha' moments in history, business, and science. These 'lightning bolt' or 'light bulb' occurrences nominally come about after many hours of research and applied study into a particular topic.

I know that is how it usually works in my writing and program creation activities. I research, read my brain out, and take copious notes, long before I ever start writing. Then I edit, have other people read and edit, and rewrite. Then I publish and take a breather.

19

Innovative ideas are sometimes 'mined' from lessons drawn from past failures. Consider **Thomas Edison** and the thousands of attempts to find a sustainable material for the filament for a light bulb.

Take the time to conduct systematic and well-rounded research, coupled with 'mining' the lessons learned from your errors and mistakes. This will help fill your mind with the raw materials necessary for creative process development. This is, as you guessed, the 'perspiration' part of the creative process and it takes an active investment on your part.

During the 'incubation' period, let your subconscious mind chew on all this material. Let it forge new and varied connections with the seemingly unrelated bits of information. Your subconscious will then send these vague feelings or intuitions to the surface or conscious mind. The creative leader knows to capture these random thoughts, however vague, impractical, or wild, for later evaluation and analysis.

Be open and accessible to all ideas – regardless of size

I've seen many people fall into the trap of waiting for the 'big idea' – a completely novel idea for a product, project, or service. They sit and wait for sudden inspiration or brilliant flashes of insight. Many are still waiting. Focusing on big ideas, we can easily become blinded from seeing smaller, otherwise 'good' and 'valuable' solutions.

*Like the story I heard of an employee in the **GAP** mailroom who noticed several packages being couriered to the same address. He checked into it, compiled them into one package with instructions on distribution at the receiving end. His 'small' change in process saved his company tens of thousands of dollars each year.*

While not as flashy or showy, these smaller insights and innovative ideas often represent very workable and profitable options. Some can even lay the foundation for other great ideas or new products and services.

Encourage your team to capture or share their ideas with you and investigate all of the options contained. Consider that the 'original' idea for the $1 billion dollar a year, **Levi Strauss** Dockers line came from one of their employees in Argentina (who worked on the docks).

Time to sweat – perspiration activities

What can you do to fertilize your mind for enhanced brainstorming, or thunder thinking, as I like to call it? *(Thunder thinking™ – when lightning strikes!)*

What kind of research or mental preparation or 'perspiration' activities will help you and your fellow leaders and professionals?

Ideas applied successfully by creative thinkers

- Visit authoritative web sites and learn how to use search engines to conduct in-depth on-line research
- Challenge your existing assumptions and mindsets. No sacred cows!
- Use Google's news alert program to keep you informed on selected areas (other search engines and web-based programs will provide this type of material, often daily.) I have several news topics on leadership, creativity, and innovation and get emails with links to those stories daily. Visit: **www.ideaman.net** Primes my pump!
- Read books and magazine articles on the topic you are studying.
- Map out the information you need and potential sources where you might find it. Then go looking!
- Ask carefully crafted open-ended questions to draw out or elicit the most usable and rich information of experts in the

area of your study. They will often be able to 'kick start' your creativity, give you a heads up, and advance your process to the next level.

- Don't be afraid to ask seemingly stupid questions – there aren't any!
- Learn to apply the four-step creative process to fully explore your ideas: preparation, incubation, illumination, and, of course, implementation or taking-action on the idea.

In the mid 80's I belonged to 'The Entrepreneurs Association'

Our Association Credo was:

"I do not choose to be a common man (or woman). It is my right to be uncommon if I can.

I seek opportunity, not security! I do not wish to be a kept citizen, humbled, and dulled by having the state look after me.

I want to take the calculated risk, to dream and to build, to fail and to succeed. I refuse to barter incentive for a dole. I prefer the challenges of life to the guaranteed existence, the thrill of fulfillment to the stale calm of utopia.

I will not trade freedom for beneficence, nor my dignity for a handout. I will NEVER cower before any master, nor bend to any threat.

It is my heritage to stand erect, proud, and unafraid; to think and act for myself, to enjoy the benefit of my creations and to face the world boldly and say, *'This with God's help, I have done.'* *All this is what it means to be an Entrepreneur."*

Entrepreneur Magazine *was initially our Association publication.*

The 21st Century version of the 3 R's

When my mom went to school, the **3 Rs used to be: reading, writing and 'rithmetic.** We need to redefine them to deal with the complex challenges we face today. Many innovations are not 'entirely' new; in fact, many represent new combinations, applications, or modifications of current, existing services, products, technologies, or materials.

I've done this with my writing and programs by drawing from previous programs or writing (articles, books) in the creation of something more adaptive or relevant to my audiences. In fact, we drew from some of our other publications, class notes, surveys, and resources for our revamped 6th edition of '*Why Didn't I THINK of That?*' and this mini-*CREATE!* edition.

Not re-inventing the wheel each time but taking it a step up or further in the development of its use and scope is a good way to 'leverage your time' and expertise. Fortunately, computers, word processing, visual outlining, or diagramming programs make it easier to gather, analyze, and manipulate information fragments into new combinations or versions for use.

This allows you to apply **these 21st Century 3 Rs in your creative process**.

- **Research**, retrieve, and record information.
- **Review** and revise the information you gather.
- **Recombine** or re-use ideas – make new associations between the idea fragments of information you've gathered.

Tips to help facilitate your creative process

With the proper preparation, any one of your team members can experience an 'ah-ha' moment. Properly applied, each team member can accomplish it. It takes training, but it is not something only an Einstein would be able to do.

Know where to look for information. Love learning – become a sponge for information on your topic or field of study. Develop the skill of asking incisive, well thought-out, open-ended questions that draw out the information, the insights, and the wisdom of those you approach.

Experiment with mind mapping or other right brain stimulation tools to map out your assumptions, questions, insights, concerns, and needs for more information.

During the interim (time delay or pause) between your 'Thunder-thinking'™ and specific brainstorming sessions, remain open for additional insights. Be a mental sponge starting with your industry or profession and flowing outward, upward, into cross-functional disciplines, business, social, or other areas. The insight you seek may not be found in the place you live or work, but it is out there.

Cultivate an 'insight-outlook'. Be open to considering information, insights, trends, and other data mined from multiple perspectives and personal experience. Work to identify and understand the inferences, underlying trends or connections they may contain and how they might pertain or impact what you are working on in your study.

Theodore Roosevelt, who was often criticized, wrote, *"It is not the critic who counts, not the man who points out how the strong man stumbled, or where the doer of deeds could have done them better. The CREDIT belongs to the man (or woman) who is actually in the arena, who strives valiantly – who knows the great enthusiasm, the great devotion ... and spends himself (or herself) in a worthy cause. Who at best, knows the triumph of high achievement; and at the worst, if he (or she) fails... at least fails while daring greatly, so that his (or her) place shall never be with those cold and timid souls... who know neither victory nor defeat."* (PS: don't let the negative or the critics distract you.)

So, you have a problem… that's great!

So, you have a problem, that's great! Whoa? Some of you are thinking, *"Are you crazy?"* Actually… NO! Someone once told me that **"I'd get paid or determine my value, by my ability to solve problems"**.

If it was that 'easy', everyone would be doing it, and the competition would be intense. But, as most customers will tell you, most businesses are not in the problem-solving field. Your ability to solve your client's problems will be directly related to the number of sales and continued growth of your firm. The more successfully and **creatively you solve these problems**, the more referrals, and fans you'll see. The more productive you are personally in being a solution-oriented owner, manager, or employee, the more dramatically it will impact your paycheck and career path.

I've learned a **simple 4-stage process for dealing with problems**. This is an effective way to deal creatively with customer complaints and concerns as well as other areas of your business and life. These ideas also work with creative and strategic planning or in everyday problem solving.

Since many of my clients and audiences have a need to be effective in dealing with their clients or customers, I've written from that perspective.

1. Invest time making sure you **UNDERSTAND** the problem.
2. The key to understanding is to **IDENTIFY** the real cause.
3. Take time to fully explore and **DISCUSS** possible solutions.
4. Take action to **SOLVE** or resolve the problem.

Creative client engagement is a commitment to go through this process with your clients. After the problem has been successfully resolved, **go the extra mile**. By that I mean do something unexpected to assist the client or to show them you appreciate the opportunity to fix the problem and prove your commitment to his well-being. This will help turn an angry or frustrated client into a fan or better yet a champion for you and your business.

Stage One: Understanding the problem. Often a problem is a perception of a difference between what we expected to happen and what happened. Here are three action steps to help.

1. Gather **ALL** the facts. Be thorough and investigate. Let the client talk!
2. Listen carefully and don't be defensive. Wait until they've finished talking and ask more questions to draw them out to find out their **REAL** concerns.
3. Rephrase or repeat the problem back to the client to make sure you've heard it correctly and understand what needs to be resolved. Agree at this stage.

It's important at this point to ensure you don't fall into the trap of denying or trying to avoid the problem. Don't blame or attack someone else. Don't demonstrate the same negative emotions in response to a customer's complaint. Just listen and calmly gather the facts!

Stage Two: Identify the Cause of the Problem. You might ask yourself or your client a few questions to find out what may have caused the problem.

1. **What has happened?** Listen and ask questions. Undertake a true assessment of the current situation.
2. **What should have happened?** Ask questions and listen carefully. Was perception a problem?
3. **What went wrong?** This is where you start partnering with the client.

Keep in mind the true cost of an unhappy client. What future purchases could you expect from this client? What future business could this client influence? What does the problem at hand cost to rectify?

Problems generally often fall into 4 major areas:

1. **Mechanics or Function** – product or service failed to work as expected.
2. **Assembly or use** – someone didn't use it correctly or put it together incorrectly.
3. **The People Factor** – we make mistakes in how we do something or how we deal with a client.
4. **Client EGO** – how this PROBLEM makes them look (good or bad) in their eyes and the eyes of their friends and families.

Stage Three: Explore and DISCUSS possible solutions.
This is possibly the most critical part in the client satisfaction/problem solving process. Here is where we need to fully focus and objectively view the challenges, we've partnered with the client to solve. **Here are three action steps.**

1. **Suggested options.** Take time to explore ALL the options that might effectively help solve this problem or at least minimize the impact.
2. **Ask your customers for their ideas.** Very often, they have a solution in mind or have some good input that will help you mutually resolve it to their satisfaction. If they are a partner in the decision, they will help make it work and will be more inclined to be happy with the results. Their satisfaction will result in referrals for you!
3. **Agree on the best solution or course of action.** After you've fully explored the options, make sure you both agree on what you will do and when to resolve it. THEN DO IT!

Stage Four: Take ACTION to resolve the problem. This is the completion stage that builds a foundation for a potential long-term relationship with your 'formerly' dissatisfied client. Make this a priority focus for your firm. Once you've agreed on what needs to be done, move heaven and earth to do it and do it better and quicker than you've promised.

Remember, they are watching to make sure you were serious about making them happy. This is your chance to 'prove' your commitment. **Again, three simple action steps.**

1. Physically remove the cause of the problem and/or take steps to retrain if it involves personnel.
2. Take corrective action to substitute, replace, or repair the product or service.
3. Ask the client if they are satisfied with the changes and action you've taken.

Go the extra mile! This is where you cement the relationship by doing something extra, something totally unexpected by the client. Show them you care and are concerned about the inconvenience they've experienced.

Use your complaints as a source of product or service development. Each one is an opportunity for you to learn how to better serve your clients, refine your service, or improve your product in the marketplace.

This is also an opportunity to expand your business or service by using solutions as steppingstones or business building blocks.

Yesterday's problems were today's new creations and improved products or services. Want to be a creative leader? Then learn from each lesson your clients give you. This is an opportunity for you to build a strong foundation for success. **Don't miss the lesson. It might be a 'v-e-r-y' valuable one!**

We explore how to enhance your creativity in more depth in 'Why Didn't I THINK of That?' available from www.SuccessPublications.ca Visit today to order your own copy and tap into your creative genius as you profitably move forward.

Take advantage of growth opportunities

At its essence, business is based on innovation, solving problems, value-added service; fulfilling the needs, wants, and desires of our clients. Here's a potpourri sampler of how to take advantage of opportunities to build or unlock your business potential by adding to the options, services, and product mix you offer your customers.

What business are you REALLY in? Keep asking this question and keep adapting your business to keep it fresh. Hint: think in terms of customer benefits. What do your clients get when they deal with you? What do they really want? Think **Airbnb** (San Francisco) who are rapidly overtaking top ranked hotels to become the world's top lodging chain.

Combine two or more products or services to create an innovative new one. Perhaps you can work with a strategic partner or ally to develop a new service or product that will bring mutual benefit! Think **Kraft** Dinner!

Take an idea from another industry and transfer it or adapt to suit yours and the needs of your clients. (For example: air miles/coffee cards/buy 10 get one free promotion.) Want to share your car and pick up some extra income? Register it on **RelayRides** or **Sidecar.**

Try something that didn't work the FIRST time. It might now; with changes in technology, resources, client needs, cultures, and attitudes.

Take advantage of the trends or changing interest in the marketplace. This is where your customer service focus will help, a lot! Think crowdsourcing!

Use a different material or process to do a traditional job. Creativity counts – it can multiply!

Look for ways to be a **value-added** company or person, focusing on real customer service. How can you personally make changes to what you bring to your work?

Being creative is often as simple as being willing to take risks by trying new or unfamiliar things and activities. Creativity is what solves your problems and builds your long-term business. Looking at your business with fresh eyes and from different perspectives is one secret in **delivering true value-added customer service.**

A personal note from Bob

I trust we've been able to share creative approaches to problem solving or strategic planning here in **'CREATE!'** I appreciate the opportunity to exercise my creativity and learn together with my audiences. Often, the lessons we discuss, and the ideas generated help me refine my approach and programs.

I would challenge you to use these tips and techniques in your day-to-day operations, as well as in your personal life. I trust you'll find them helpful.

Remember there is 'always' a creative solution! Share these ideas with your clients and co-workers, so they can take advantage of ways to make their lives more productive and less stressful. As you continue to read and re-read, focus on the ones that might serve you best as you begin to reframe your approach to problems that inevitably appear in your life and career. I hope you enjoy it.

One of the challenges of speaking within a time frame and having a topic that has so many variables to discuss is covering the most relevant material. That is one of the reasons for developing these books and learning guides to help my audience members following a presentation.

Copyright and license notes

CREATE! *Idea-rich strategies for enhanced innovation*

Bob 'Idea Man' Hooey, Accredited Speaker, 2011 Spirit of CAPS recipient. Prolific author of 30 plus business, leadership, and career success publications

Photos of Bob: **Dov Friedman**, www.photographybyDov.com
Bonnie-Jean McAllister, www.elantraphotography.com
Editorial, layout and design: **Irene Gaudet,** Vitrak Creative Services, vitrakcreative.com

ISBN: 9781998014125

Printed in the United States 10 9 8 7 6 5 4 3 2 1
Success Publications – a division of Creativity Corner Inc.
Box 10, Egremont, AB T0A 0Z0
www.successpublications.ca
Creative office: 1-780-736-0009

"An idea is a feat of association." Robert Frost

Acknowledgements, credits, and disclaimers

תודה
Dankie **Gracias**
Спасибо شكراً **Takk**
Merci
Köszönjük Terima kasih
Grazie Dziękujemy Děkojame
Ďakujeme Vielen Dank **Paldies**
Kiitos Täname teid 謝謝

Thank You
Tak

感謝您 Obrigado Teşekkür Ederiz
감사합니다
Σας Ευχαριστούμ ขอบคุณ
Bedankt **Děkujeme vám**
ありがとうございます
Tack

As with each of my books, a very special dedication of this piece of myself, to the two people who meant the most to me, my folks **Ron and Marge Hooey**. Sadly, both my parents left this earthly realm in 1999. I still miss our time together and your encouragement and love. I was blessed with the two of you in my life. I've added **George and Lillian Sidor** (Irene's folks) to this gratitude list.

To my inspiring wife and professional proofreader and publications coach, **Irene Gaudet,** who loves, encourages, and supports me in my quest to continue sharing my **Ideas At Work!** across the world. Thank you seems so inadequate for your timely work in helping make my writing and my client service better! I love the time we spend together!

To my colleagues and friends in Toastmasters, the National Speakers Association (NSA), the Canadian Association of Professional Speakers (CAPS), and the Global Speakers Federation (GSF) who continually challenge me to strive for success and increased excellence.

To my great audiences, leaders, students, coaching clients, and readers across the globe who share their experiences and enjoyment of my work. Your positive and supportive feedback encourages me to keep working on additional programs and success publications like this updated version. My experience with you creates the foundation for additional real-life experiences I can take from the stage to the page, the classroom to the boardroom.

My thanks to a select few friends for your ongoing support and 'constructive' abuse. You know who you are. ☺

Disclaimer

We have not attempted to cite all the authorities and sources consulted in the preparation of this book. To do so would require much more space than is available. The list would include departments of various governments, libraries, industrial institutions, periodicals, and many individuals. Inspiration was drawn from many sources, including other books by the author; in this updated creation of this min-version of **'CREATE!'**

'Create!'' is written and designed to provide information on more creative use of your time, as a business leader's enhancement guide. It is sold with the 'explicit' understanding that the publisher and/or the author are not engaged in rendering legal, accounting, or other Professional services. If legal or other expert assistance is required, the services of a competent Professional in your geographic area should be sought.

It is not the purpose of this mini book to reprint all the information that is otherwise available. Its primary purpose is to complement, amplify, and supplement other books and reference materials already available. You are encouraged to search out and study all the available material, learn as much as possible, and tailor the information to your individual needs. This will help to enhance your success in being a more effective salesperson, leader or professional.

Every effort has been made to make this book as complete and as accurate as possible within the scope of its focus. However, there may be mistakes, both typographical and in content or attribution. Graphics are royalty free or under license. Care has been taken to trace ownership of copyright material contained in this volume. The publisher will gladly receive information that will allow him to rectify any reference or credit line in subsequent editions. This book should be used only as a general guide and not as the ultimate source of information. Furthermore, this book contains information that is current only up to the date of publication.

The purpose of 'Create!' is to educate and entertain; *perhaps to inform and to inspire. It is certainly to challenge its readers to learn and apply its secrets and tips, to challenge them to enhance their skills and leverage their efforts to create more Productive outcomes. The author and publisher shall have neither liability nor responsibility to any person or entity with respect to any loss or damage caused, or alleged to have been caused, directly or indirectly, by the information contained in this book.*

Bob's B.E.S.T. publications

Bob is a *prolific* author who has been capturing and sharing his wisdom and experience in print and electronic formats for the past fifteen plus years. In addition to the following publications, several of them best sellers, he has written for consumer, corporate, trade, professional associations, and on-line publications. He has been engaged to write and assist on publications by other best-selling writers and successful companies.

Bob's **B**usiness **E**nhancement **S**uccess **T**ools

Leadership, business, and career success series
Running TOO Fast (8th edition 2022)
Legacy of Leadership (6th edition 2024)
Make ME Feel Special! (6th edition 2022)
Why Didn't I 'THINK' of That? (5th edition 2022)
Speaking for Success! (10th edition 2023)
THINK Beyond the First Sale (3rd edition 2022)
Prepare Yourself to WIN! (3rd edition 2018)

Bob's mini-book success series
The Courage to Lead! (4th edition 2024)
Creative Conflict (3rd edition 2024)
Get to YES! (5th edition 2023)
THINK Before You Ink! (3rd edition 2017)
Running to Win! (2nd edition 2017)
Generate More Sales (5th edition 2023)
Unleash your Business Potential (3rd edition 2017)
Learn to Listen (2nd edition 2017)

Creativity Counts! (3rd edition 2024)
Create Your Future! (3rd edition 2017)

Bob's Pocket Wisdom series *(coming as e-books in 2024)*
Pocket Wisdom for **Selling Professionals**
Pocket Wisdom for **Speakers** (updated 2023)
Pocket Wisdom for **Innovators**
Pocket Wisdom for **Leaders – Power of One!** (updated 2023)
Pocket Wisdom for **Business Builders**

Co-authored books created by Bob
Quantum Success – 3 volume series (2006)
In the Company of Leaders (3rd edition 2014)
Foundational Success (2nd edition 2013)

Bob's Idea-rich leaders edge series (new 2018-2024)
LEAD! *12 idea-rich leadership success strategies*
CREATE! *Idea-rich strategies for enhanced innovation*
TIME! *Idea-rich tips for enhanced performance and productivity*
SERVE! *Idea-rich strategies for enhanced customer service*
SPEAK! *Idea-rich tips and techniques for great presentations*
CREATIVE CONFLICT *Idea-rich leadership for team success*

More to come in 2024

Visit: www.SuccessPublications.ca for more information on Bob's publications and other success resources.

Email: bob@ideaman.net or visit:
www.SuccessPublications.ca

"Innovation is a learned skill of
observation and application –
Ideas At Work!"
Bob 'Idea Man' Hooey
'My 'NEXT' Million Dollar Idea Book'

What they say about Bob 'Idea Man' Hooey

I frequently travel across North America, and more recently around the globe, sharing my **Ideas At Work!**

I am fortunate to get feedback and comments from my audiences and colleagues. These comments come from people who have been touched, challenged, or simply enjoyed themselves in one of my sessions.

"I still get comments from people about your presentation. Only a few speakers have left an impression that lasts that long. You hit a spot with the tourism people." **Janet Bell**, Yukon Economic Forums

*"**Thank you, Bob**, it is always a pleasure to see a true professional at work. You have made the name 'Speaker' stand out as a truism - someone who encourages people to examine their lives and adjust. The comments indicated you hit people right where it is important - in their hearts. Each of those in your audience took away a new feeling of personal success and encouragement."* **Sherry Knight**, Dimension Eleven Human Resources and Communications

*"I am pleased to recommend **Bob 'Idea Man' Hooey** to any organization looking for a charismatic, confident speaker and seminar leader. I have seen Bob in action on several occasions, and he is ALWAYS on! Bob has the ability to grab his audience's attention and keep it. Quite simply, if Bob is involved - your program or seminar is guaranteed to succeed."* **Maurice Laving**, Coordinator Training and Development, London Drugs

*"On very short notice Bob cleared his schedule and graciously presented at our meeting when the original Speaker was unable to attend. **Last week Bob set the tone for our two-day leadership meeting and gave us all a motivational lift.** His compassion and true interest in people was clearly evident, making him very credible. He shared some great stories, has a wealth of experience and knowledge and it was a pleasure listening to him. His down-to-Earth style makes it easier to retain the information presented. He also followed up with additional info and handouts, cementing his message of building bridges, not walls. Fantastic job, Bob, and thanks again!"* **Barbara Afra Beler**, MBA, Senior Specialist Commercial Community, Alberta North, **BMO Bank of Montreal**

"I have been so excited working with Bob Hooey, as he has given inspiration and motivation to our leadership team members. Both at the Brick Warehouse – Alberta and here at Art Van Furniture – Michigan; with his years of experience in working with business executives and his humorous and delightful packaging of his material, he makes learning with Bob a real joy. But most importantly, anyone who encounters his material is the better for it."
Kim Yost, CEO Art Van Furniture, former CEO The Brick

Motivate your teams, your employees, and your leaders to 'productively' grow and 'profitably' succeed!

Protect your conference investment - leverage your training dollars.

Enhance your professional career and sell more products and services.

Equip and motivate your leaders and their teams to grow and succeed, 'even' in tough times!

Leverage your time to enhance your skills, equip your teams, and better serve your clients.

Leverage your leadership and investment of time to leave a significant legacy!

Call today to engage best-selling author, award winning, inspirational leadership keynote speaker, leaders' success coach, and employee development trainer, **Bob 'Idea Man' Hooey** and his innovative, audience based, results-focused, **Ideas At Work!** for your next company, convention, leadership, staff, training, or association event. You'll be glad you did!

Call 1-780-736-0009 to connect with Bob 'Idea Man' Hooey today!

Learn more about Bob at:
www.ideaman.net or
www.BobHooey.training

Synergy revived

Synergy has a number of applications in our lives, our careers, and our businesses

Synergy as a driver or operating efficiencies: revisiting the re-engineering concept to see what changes can still be made to assist in making your processes more effective or streamlined.

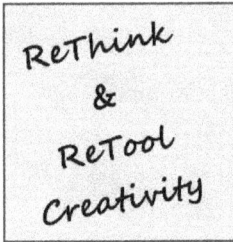

Synergy in marketing: for example, the use of cross platform campaigns by media companies to explore their motion picture, publishing, and merchandising properties. Disney and The Lion King used this strategy to go from $50 million to $3 Billion in total revenues.

ReThink & ReTool Creativity

Synergy as a transformational strategy for business.

- MTV – a blend of cable TV and pre-recorded music.
- Computer video games – descended from earlier board games, arcade games, and PC connections. Thousands of new Apps to download.
- Netflix – replaced the local video store. Blogs replacing traditional media.
- TiVo – video on demand (private TV station) Also, think **YouTube**!
- **Roy Speer** and **Lowell Paxson** noticed people liked shopping and watching TV. The Home Shopping Network, a 24-hour shopping channel, was launched.
- Internet shopping – **Amazon** – you can shop and ship around the world.

Synergy works because it mirrors how we now live. How are you equipped to creatively use it?

www.ingramcontent.com/pod-product-compliance
Lightning Source LLC
Chambersburg PA
CBHW071525210326
41597CB00018B/2905